THE LITTLE BOOK OF BEER TIPS

ANDREW LANGLEY

22

Beef carbonnade of Northern France is the most famous of all beer dishes.

Soften onions in oil, then brown 1kg (2lb) of lean beef in slices and remove. Into the pan put 2 teaspoons of sugar and 2 tablespoons of flour. Add 500ml (1 pint) of dark beer and reduce. Layer meat and onions in a dish, pour over the liquid and cook in a low oven for 3 hours.

21

North American settlers of old discovered that **beer makes better bread dough.** Mix up your customary yeast dough recipe (preferably with a little rye flour). In place of part of the water, add 250ml ($^1/_2$ pint) of flat beer, slightly warmed, as well as a beaten egg and a teaspoon of ground coriander seed. Knead and bake as usual.

20

Try a lambic beer.

Made almost exclusively in Belgium, this is one of the most unusual beer styles in the world. The newly-made brew is left in an open tank, where it picks up wild yeast microbes from the air. The long and unique fermentation process produces a wonderfully fruity and complex flavour.

THE LITTLE BOOK OF BEER TIPS

ANDREW LANGLEY

A.
Absolute Press

First published in Great Britain in 2006 by
Absolute Press
Scarborough House, 29 James Street West
Bath BA1 2BT, England
Phone 44 (0) 1225 316013 **Fax** 44 (0) 1225 445836
E-mail info@absolutepress.co.uk
Web www.absolutepress.co.uk

A catalogue record of this book is available from the British Library

ISBN: 190457338X
ISBN 13: 9781904573470

Printed and bound in Italy by Legoprint

‘For a quart of ale is a dish for a king.’

Autolycus,
***A Winter’s Tale*, Shakespeare**

1

Enjoy as many different beers
of the world
as you can.

No other drink offers such a staggering variety – weak or strong, dark or pale, bitter or sweet, fruity or hoppy. The beers of Britain, Belgium, Bavaria, the USA, Scandinavia, Australia, Japan, India and dozens of other lands all have their own styles and peculiarities. Be adventurous.

2

In a bar, pub or beer shop

always go for the local beer

if possible. Look out for beer which has been brewed nearby. This way you will discover new, exciting and sometimes esoteric tastes. Local brews usually reflect local conditions. (And, whatever they say, cask-conditioned beer does not generally travel well).

3

Build up your own bottled beer cellar

(a cupboard will do). The possible range is vast, of course, so concentrate on collecting a wide variety of types (lagers, stouts, pale ales and so on). Buy any unusual or exceptional brew you come across on your travels.

4

Keep your beer in a dark place.

Sunlight and other bright light causes a reaction in the beer's hop acids which can produce a nasty sulphurous smell. The clear or green glass of most beer bottles encourages this process.

5

Pouring bottled beers is an art

– but the rules are few and simple. Tilt the glass to no less than 45%. Keep the mouth of the bottle on or near the lower lip of the glass. Pour the beer slowly and smoothly to prevent excessive foaming. As the glass fills, gradually bring it back to upright.

6

Some bottled beers contain a yeasty sediment (which means that it is still fermenting – very slowly – in the bottle). This can make the beer cloudy, but remember:

yeast is good for you. You can let the bottle stand for a while and then pour it out with excessive care. However, the sediment won't do you any harm – quite the opposite, in fact.

7

Warmth will make most bottled beers go stale.

Store beers at low temperatures

to slow down the oxidation process.
This can react with the fatty acids and other delicate chemicals in the beer to develop harsh tastes and an aroma like damp cardboard.

8

The vast majority of bottled beers are made to be drunk within a few weeks. However, **some beers** will improve with age and **can be laid down like good wines.**

These will develop over two years or more in the bottle. The granddaddy of them is the sublime Thomas Hardy's Ale, which goes on maturing for up to 25 years.

9

Always check on a beer's alcohol content. This varies hugely across the range. The content should be displayed on the pump, bottle or can, and is shown as a percentage of alcohol by volume. Most ordinary draught beers are around 4–5%, but the stronger stuff in bottles soars up to over 10% (the world record is somewhere in the mid-20s!).

10

Low strength beers can be just as tasty and interesting as the harder stuff. So be adaptable in your choice, and

suit the beer to the occasion.

Drink the stronger brews in the depths of winter or before and after a meal. But if you're spending time in a bar or pub in warm weather, stick to the weaker beers.

11

Inspect the colour and clarity of a beer. If served in a bar or pub, it should be crystal-clear (except in a very few special cases). Send back any draught beer which is cloudy or dull-looking. Your beer's colour can be a thing of beauty, ranging from nocturnal black through all shades of brown to straw-yellow, so make the most of it.

12

Whether it's from barrel or bottle,

always give the beer a thorough sniff

before you take the first sip. The aroma of a beer is a key part of your enjoyment. You should be able to smell hops, malt and (maybe) yeast, plus any of a host of other qualities. Take time to identify them. Anything reeking of bad eggs should be avoided, however.

13

Swill the first sip around your mouth gently.

This will allow you to feel the 'body', or weightiness, of the brew. It will also, of course, allow you to sense the various tastes on your tongue – sweet at the front and hoppy bitterness at the back. Savour the moment, because once you swallow the tastes are gone. There are no flavour receptors in your throat.

14

Take a good look at the beer's 'head'.

The foam should hang around, and not fizz away into nothing like lemonade. A stable head is usually produced by the malt proteins and the hop acids (though it can be boosted artificially with a dose of carbon dioxide or nitrogen). The bubbles should also cling to the glass as the level of beer recedes.

15

If you pour out beer too vigorously, how do you

stop the froth from overflowing

the top of the glass? Simply touch the rim with a finger or lip. These will leave traces of oil, which destabilize the bubbles and should cause the foam to subside. For the same reason, all glasses should be rinsed free of all oil or soap residues.

16

A chilled drink may be refreshing in hot weather,

but **be prepared for the side-effects of very cold beer.**

The cold preserves the beer's fizziness for much longer, so that the bubbles survive down into your digestive system. This can cause the stomach to become bloated – with unfortunate and sometimes painful results.

17

Serve beers at the correct temperature

to bring out the best taste. This varies according to the beer type. Top-fermented brews such as British bitter should be just under room temperature. Lagers are best at about 10°C (50°F). Anything lower than this will leave no taste at all (something which suits many beers just fine).

18

It's best to

drink beer from a clear glass.

Bottles or cans are OK for very cold drinks where flavour is not important, but decent brews should be served properly. A beer which is poured into a glass loses some of its carbon dioxide and becomes less 'prickly'. And clear glass (as opposed to pewter or china) allows you to appreciate the colour.

19

Stout goes remarkably well with mushrooms.

Gently fry about 250g (8oz) chopped mushrooms in butter. Add chopped garlic, a dash of Worcestershire sauce and a pinch of salt. Finally, slosh in a wine glass of stout and reduce to thicken. Serve the mushrooms and sauce on toast.

23

Pale beer and cod – a hearty and unusual combination.

Sauté a thinly sliced onion in butter, then pour in 250ml ($^1/_2$ pint) of strong lager or pale ale. Boil off the alcohol and reduce. Add a couple of skinned cod fillets. Cover and cook more gently for 15 minutes. Serve with floury boiled potatoes.

24

Just for good measure, here's

another great fish and beer recipe.

It is a variation on the usual fish-and-chip batter. Mix 250g (8oz) seasoned plain flour with 2 tablespoons sunflower oil and 250ml ($^1/_2$ pint) of bitter and leave to mature for 1 hour. Add a little more beer, plus whipped egg whites, coat the fish (cod, haddock, coley) and deep-fry.

25

A strong ale Christmas pudding exploits the contrast between the bitterness of hops and the sweetness of dried fruit. To each 1kg (2lb) of dry ingredients, add about 200ml (7 fl oz) of good meaty beer or stout, plus a measure of whisky. Then proceed in the usual way.

26

On a cold night, **beer can be heated or 'mulled' and flavoured with spices.** First, boil up a syrup of 125g (4oz) sugar and the juice of 5 oranges and 3 lemons. Warm 2 litres (4 pints) of strong winter ale with cinnamon, nutmeg and a big wine glass of dry sherry. Stir in (strained) syrup and serve – but not too hot, or the alcohol will evaporate.

27

Lamb's wool is the classic wassail drink for Christmas Eve

(from the Anglo-Saxon 'waes hael', meaning 'good health'). Roast 8 apples until soft. Gently warm 2 litres (4 pints) of bitter beer with 2 cinnamon sticks, 10 cloves and a chunk of peeled ginger. Remove the spices, whisk in 4 whipped egg yolks and 250ml ($^1/_2$ pint) cream, and pop in the apples.

28

The oldest method of mulling winter ale is to warm a poker in the fire and then plunge it into the beer. Try it at least once because it has an astonishing effect. The beer foams up and gives off a lovely malty aroma. And, as you drink, you suck up the cool beer beneath the warmed head (like Irish coffee in reverse).

29

Stout and oysters is a perfect marriage – the thick, dry bitterness of the stout matches brilliantly the thin, salty mystery of the oyster. Guinness is fine, but experiment with even classier alternatives.

30

Get rid of beer stains as soon as possible.

Wet stains on carpets or upholstery should be dabbed with a paper towel, then sprayed with a mixture of clear vinegar and water and dabbed again. For a dry stain, spray with diluted washing up liquid. Still not clean? Spray on a little hydrogen peroxide in water and leave for 30 minutes.

31

Try (at least once) a 'dog's nose'.

This strange cocktail, mentioned by both Charles Dickens and Elizabeth Gaskell, creates a fascinating combination of tastes. Gently warm 250ml ($^1/_2$ pint) of porter or stout with sugar and nutmeg, then add a generous measure of gin.

32

Beer makes an excellent marinade for some meats

(and even some fish). Stewing steak and lamb shoulder are the most obvious candidates, but the lesser game animals benefit even more. Marinate jointed hare or rabbit in strong ale laced with bay leaves, black peppercorns and a sliced onion.

33

Danish lager is an integral part of a Danish fondue. Gently brown a chopped onion and 4 chopped rashers of lean bacon in butter. Mix in 3 tablespoons of plain flour, cook for a minute then gradually add 250ml ($^{1}/_{2}$ pint) of lager. Stir until it thickens. Finally grate in 450g (1lb) of cheese (Havarti, Gruyère or Gjetost). Serve with gherkins and chunks of bread.

34

On warm summer evenings,

refresh yourself with a cold beer soup.

Soak 2 tablespoons of raisins for 30 minutes in a slug of eau-de-vie. Then mix in the crumbs from a slice of wholemeal bread and $^1/_2$ litre (1 pint) of good quality lager. Leave for another 10 minutes, then eat with cream and sugar to taste.

35

Strong ale is the perfect partner for cheese.

Cheeses are a complex food, with a huge range of texture and acidity. A beer with a lot of fruity, malty flavours helps to accentuate the sharpness of some cheeses and the creaminess of others.

36

Many creatures adore beer –
even the humble garden slug. So you can
lure these **pests to an inebriated death** with beer slug traps.
Sink bowls or saucers to their rims in the soil and fill up with flat beer. The slugs will be drawn as if by a magnet.

37

Transform the humble spud with a pale ale dressing.

Soften a chopped onion in oil, then add 125ml ($^1/_4$ pint) of a good pale ale, 3 tablespoons of cider vinegar and a teaspoon of sugar. Reduce, then beat in 1 tablespoon of wholegrain mustard and more oil to taste. Season and pour over hot boiled potatoes mixed with fried onions.

38

Chosen imaginatively, beer can be incorporated in any course of a meal. **Try a beer fruit cup,** which combines a scoop of fruit sorbet with a good helping of fruit beer and a sprinkling of fresh fruit. A Belgian framboise would do very well.

39

Hops and Hogmanay:

Haggis is a grainy dish from a grain-growing land. Served properly, with mashed swede and potato, it cries out to be washed down with a grainy drink. A fine hoppy bitter – preferably Scottish – will suit it much better than wine.

40

It's true! **A beer rinse can add shine and bounce to your hair.** After washing, conditioning and rinsing your hair as normal, try rinsing it again in a can or bottle of light beer. Wait five minutes and then wash it out.

41

Beer and cheese make fine cooking partners, and Welsh rabbit (not rarebit) is their most famous party piece. Gently warm a good chunk of butter, and stir in 4 tablespoons of brown ale, 125g (8oz) of grated Cheshire cheese and a dash of Worcestershire sauce. When mixed, pour onto toast and brown under the grill.

42

Loin of pork can sometimes taste a little bland.

Braise pork in beer and you highlight a host of subtleties.

Brown the pork in oil, then replace it in the pan with onions and garlic. When they're soft, put in 560ml (1 pint) hoppy beer and a bay leaf. Return the pork and cook gently for 2 hours.

43

Transform old scraps of cheese by turning them into beer-potted cheese. Grate the cheese into a bowl, and season with salt, pepper, mustard and a pinch of mace. Mix energetically with some softened butter and as much barley wine as it will soak up. Put into little pots and seal with melted butter. Spread on toast or oatcakes.

44

Plagued by wasps and other buzzing creatures when you sit outside? **Empty beer bottles and cans make excellent insect traps.**

Put a finger of waste beer in each and position them strategically round your sitting-out area. The insects, unable to resist the aroma, will crawl inside and drown.

45

Piscine Partners!

The delicate flavour of white fish can easily be swamped by a pushy drink accompaniment. Light beers, especially a German wheat beer or a dry Czech pilsner, are the perfect answer. For heftier tastes, such as smoked salmon, try a malty brown ale or a rich porter.

46

Beer is at the heart of

Carp in Black Sauce, a classic Czech recipe.

Soften chopped onions, parsnips, carrots and celeriac in butter. Add lemon juice, a dash of wine vinegar and water, and 150ml ($^1/_4$ pint) of dark ale. Simmer with peppercorns, allspice, peeled ginger and lemon peel, plus breadcrumbs and dried fruit. Top it all with thick carp steaks and cook for a further 15 minutes.

47

It may not be hoppy or alcoholic, but

nettle beer is easy, quick and cheap to make.

Boil up 2.2 litres (4 pints) of water, with a big tied bunch of fresh young nettles, 450g (1lb) of sugar, tablespoons of ground ginger and cream of tartar, plus a lemon. Strain the result into the same amount of cold water, add yeast and leave to work for 12 hours before bottling.

48

Yorkshire ale gruel makes a sturdy nightcap for winter nights. Boil a handful of oats in 280ml ($^1/_2$ pint) of water with a grated chunk of ginger. Strain it off into an equal amount of hot winter ale, adding nutmeg, cinnamon and honey. Drink while still hot and go straight to bed.

49

Add a new dimension to vegetables by cooking them in beer.

Halve Brussels sprouts and sauté with bacon and garlic before simmering in beer. Fry carrots in butter then pour on beer and cook gently with a pinch of sugar. Cabbage also responds to this treatment (add caraway seeds).

50

Dessert Beers!

As a general rule, sweet beers go well with sweet food. For creamy desserts, try an oatmeal stout, an Imperial stout or even a Belgian fruit beer. For chocolate dishes – what else but a chocolate-flavoured beer?

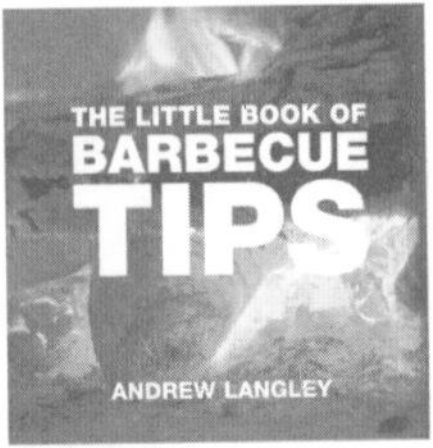
THE LITTLE BOOK OF
BARBECUE
TIPS
ANDREW LANGLEY

THE LITTLE BOOK OF
BEER
TIPS
ANDREW LANGLEY

THE LITTLE BOOK OF
HERB
TIPS
WILLIAM FORTT

THE LITTLE BOOK OF
POKER
TIPS
DAVID MITCHELL

THE LITTLE BOOK OF
GARDENING
TIPS
WILLIAM FORTT

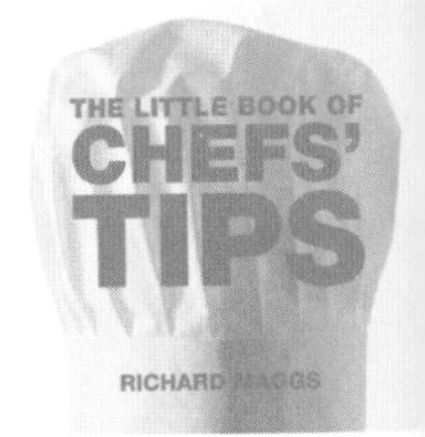
THE LITTLE BOOK OF
CHEFS'
TIPS
RICHARD MAGGS

THE LITTLE BOOK OF
SPICE
TIPS
ANDREW LANGLEY

THE LITTLE BOOK OF
GOLF
TIPS
PAUL HART

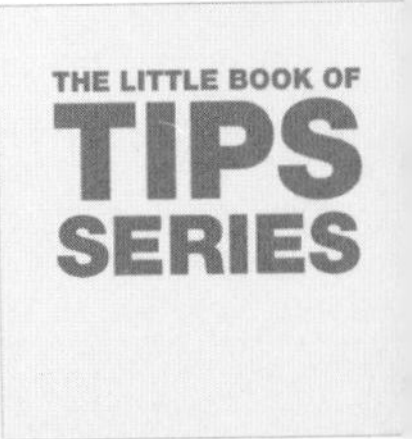
THE LITTLE BOOK OF
TIPS
SERIES

THE LITTLE BOOK OF
CHEESE
TIPS
ANDREW LANGLEY

THE LITTLE BOOK OF
WINE
TIPS
ANDREW LANGLEY

THE LITTLE BOOK OF
COFFEE
TIPS
ANDREW LANGLEY

THE LITTLE BOOK OF
TEA
TIPS
ANDREW LANGLEY

THE LITTLE BOOK OF
AGA
TIPS
RICHARD MAGGS

THE LITTLE BOOK OF
CHRISTMAS
AGA
TIPS
RICHARD MAGGS

Little Books of Tips from Absolute Press

The Little Book of Tea Tips
The Little Book of Wine Tips
The Little Book of Cheese Tips
The Little Book of Coffee Tips
The Little Book of Herb Tips
The Little Book of Gardening Tips
The Little Book of Barbecue Tips
The Little Book of Chefs' Tips
The Little Book of Spice Tips
The Little Book of Beer Tips
The Little Book of Poker Tips
The Little Book of Golf Tips
The Little Book of Aga Tips
The Little Book of Aga Tips 2
The Little Book of Aga Tips 3
The Little Book of Christmas Aga Tips
The Little Book of Rayburn Tips

Forthcoming titles:

The Little Book of Champagne Tips
The Little Book of Travel Tips
The Little Book of Cleaning Tips
The Little Book of Chocolate Tips
The Little Book of Diet Tips
The Little Book of Marmite Tips
The Little Book of Garden Design Tips
The Little Book of Container Plant Tips
The Little Book of Camping Tips
The Little Book of Puppy Tips
The Little Book of Kitten Tips

All titles: £2.99 / 112 pages